BLESSED NAMES
WHY WAS HE NAMED HASAN (A)?
WRITTEN BY:
KISA KIDS PUBLICATIONS

Please recite a Fātiḥah for the marḥūmīn
of the Rangwala family, the sponsors of this book.

All proceeds from the sale of this book
will be used to produce more educational resources.

Dedication

This book is dedicated to the beloved Imām of our time (AJ). May Allāh (swt) hasten his reappearance and help us t become his true companions.

Acknowledgements

Prophet Muḥammad (s): The pen of a writer is mightier than the blood of a martyr.

True reward lies with Allāh, but we would like to sincerely thank Shaykh Salim Yusufali and Sisters Sabika Mitha Liliana Villalvazo, Zahra Sabur, Kisae Nazar, Sarah Assaf, Nadia Dossani, Fatima Hussain, Naseem Rangwala, an Zehra Abbas. We would especially like to thank Nainava Publications for their contributions. May Allāh bless them i this world and the next.

Preface

Prophet Muḥammad (s): Nurture and raise your children in the best way. Raise them with the love of the Prophet and the Ahl al-Bayt (a).

Literature is an influential form of media that often shapes the thoughts and views of an entire generation. Therefore in order to establish an Islamic foundation for the future generations, there is a dire need for compelling Islami literature. Over the past several years, this need has become increasingly prevalent throughout Islamic centers an schools everywhere. Due to the growing dissonance between parents, children, society, and the teachings of Islār and the Ahl al-Bayt (a), this need has become even more pressing. Al-Kisa Foundation, along with its subsidiary, Kis: Kids Publications, was conceived in an effort to help bridge this gap with the guidance of ʿulamah and the help o educators. We would like to make this a communal effort and platform. Therefore, we sincerely welcome constructive feedback and help in any capacity.

The goal of the *Blessed Names* series is to help children form a lasting bond with the 14 Māʿṣūmīn by learning about and connecting with their names. We hope that you and your children enjoy these books and use them as a means to achieve this goal, inshā'Allāh. We pray to Allāh to give us the strength and tawfīq to perform our duties and responsibilities.

With Duʾās,
Nabi R. Mir (Abidi)

Kisa Kids Publications
4415 Fortran Court
San Jose, CA 95134
(260) KISA-KID [547-2543]

An Introduction to the Blessed Names

Our names are a very special part of us. Many times, they shape our personalities and even explain who we are or the person we would like to become. In this series, you will explore the names and titles of our beloved 14 Ma'soomeen. Did you know that their names and titles were not just ordinary names? They were special because they were given to them by Allah!

Allah has given seven special heavenly names to our Ma'soomeen: Muhammad, Ali, Fatimah, Hasan, Husain, Ja'far, and Musa. Behind each of these names is a heavenly power!

In addition to their names, each of the Ma'soomeen also had special titles by which they became famous. Their titles were often given to them because of the circumstances of their time, but these titles and characteristics were common amongst all the Ma'soomeen. For example, Imam al-Baqir (a) was known for spreading knowledge because he was able to create many new universities and branches of knowledge during his time. However, if the other Ma'soomeen had the same opportunity, they, too, would have spread knowledge and created universities in their teaching circles. In these stories, you will discover some of the reasons why the Ma'soomeen received their specific names or titles.

Many of us share our names with these beloved Ma'soomeen or know people who do. Let's learn about these blessed names and titles so we can strive to be like our blessed Ma'soomeen!

I think Hasan means...

_____

It was that special time of the year again — the time for worship, the time of remembrance. You could almost feel the blessings in the air. Yes, it was the holy month of Ramadhan in Medina!

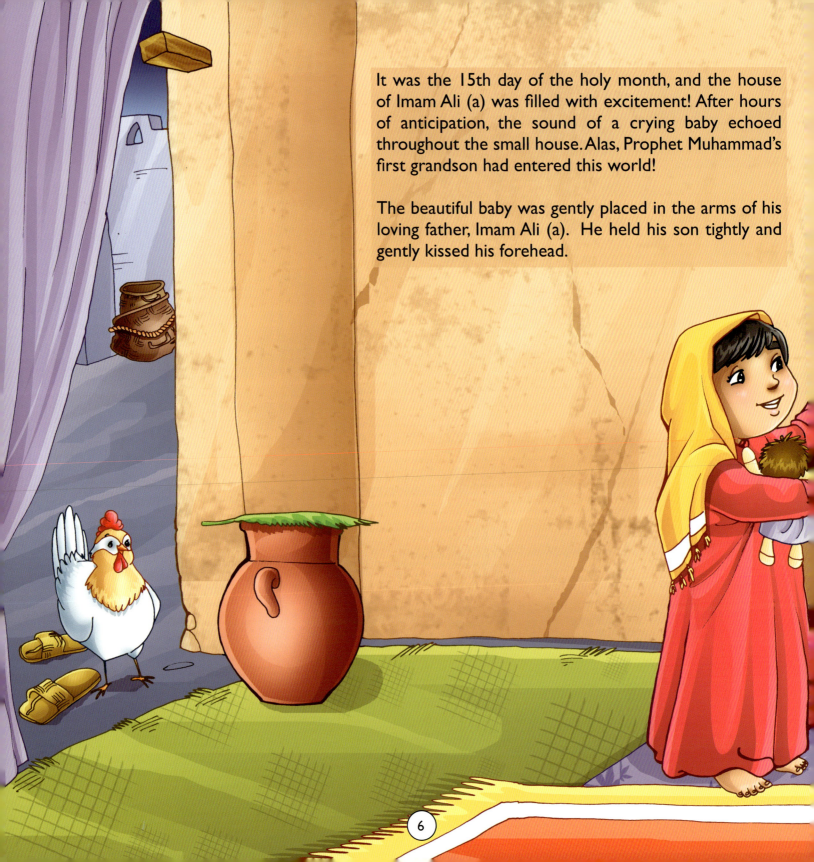

It was the 15th day of the holy month, and the house of Imam Ali (a) was filled with excitement! After hours of anticipation, the sound of a crying baby echoed throughout the small house. Alas, Prophet Muhammad's first grandson had entered this world!

The beautiful baby was gently placed in the arms of his loving father, Imam Ali (a). He held his son tightly and gently kissed his forehead.

Prophet Muhammad (s) was overjoyed seeing his beautiful grandchild. He wrapped him in a pure white blanket and asked Imam Ali (a), "What name have you chosen?"

Imam Ali (a) replied, "O Rasulullah, how can I make such an important decision without asking you first? Only the name that you choose will be given to this child."

The Prophet (s) smiled and replied, "And I will not name him without asking Allah first."

All of a sudden, a bright light shone from the sky and Angel Jibraeel descended from heaven. He greeted the Prophet (s), "Salaamun Alaikum, O Messenger of Allah! Allah sends His peace upon you and congratulates you on the birth of your beautiful grandson."

"I have come with good news! Allah wishes you to name this child Shubbar, just like the son of Prophet Haroon (a). You see, Prophet Haroon (a) was very special to his brother, Prophet Musa (a), just like Imam Ali (a) is very special to you. That is why Allah has chosen this special name for your grandson."

Prophet Muhammad (s) was overjoyed! He asked, "O Jibraeel, how do you say 'Shubbar' in Arabic?"

Jibraeel smiled and said, "Hasan."

The Prophet (s) was delighted upon hearing this beautiful name and announced to everyone in the room, "Allah has named this child Hasan! 'Hasan' means 'goodness' or the 'good-doer.'"

Everybody smiled and rejoiced when they heard the Prophet's announcement.

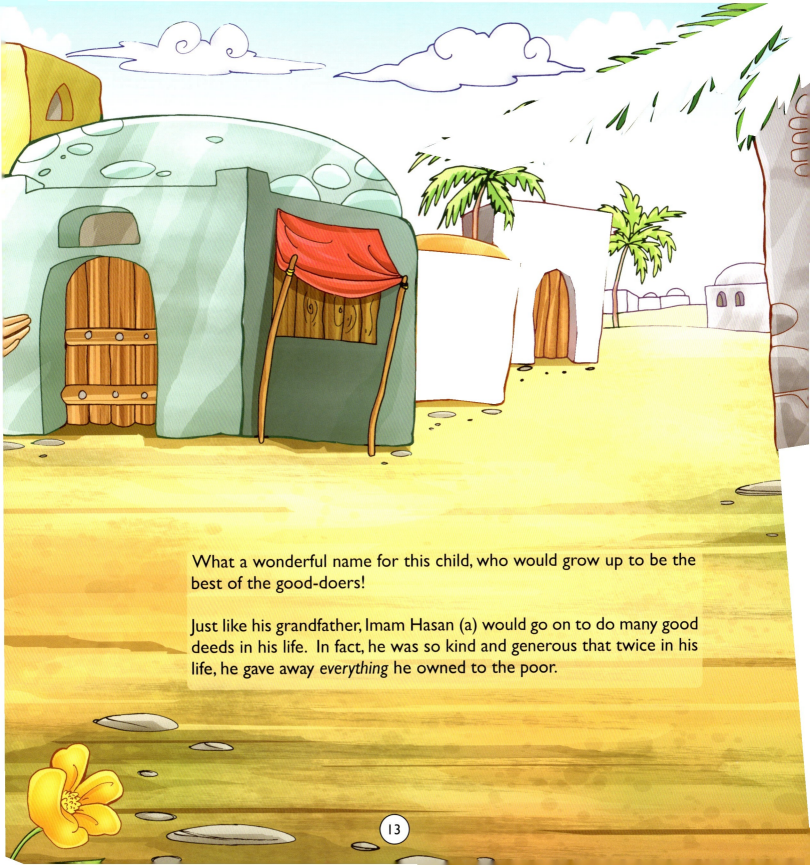

What a wonderful name for this child, who would grow up to be the best of the good-doers!

Just like his grandfather, Imam Hasan (a) would go on to do many good deeds in his life. In fact, he was so kind and generous that twice in his life, he gave away *everything* he owned to the poor.

14

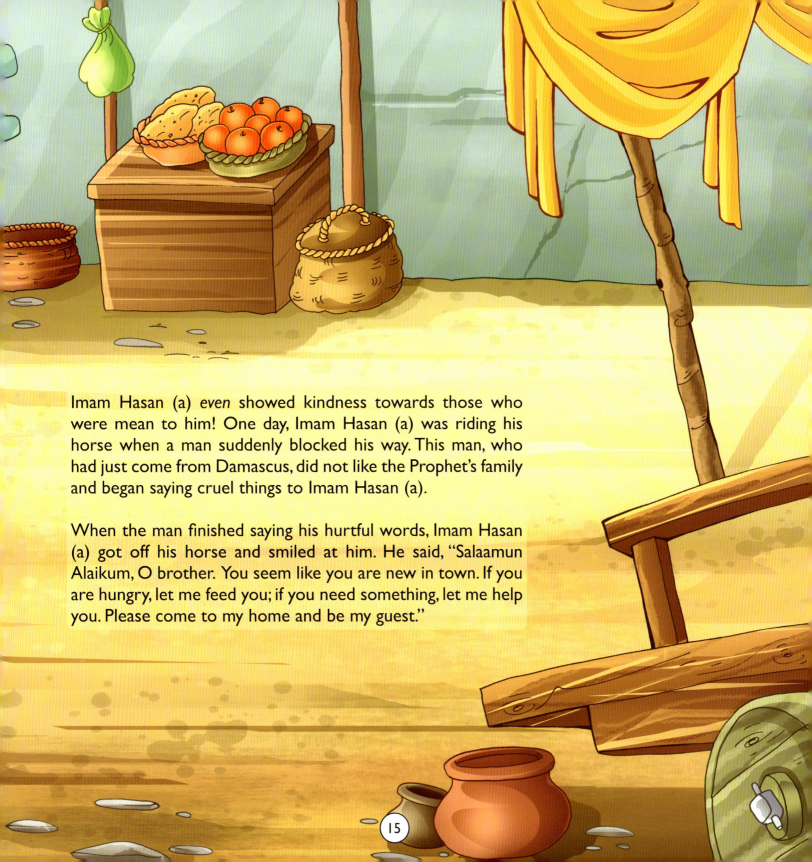

Imam Hasan (a) *even* showed kindness towards those who were mean to him! One day, Imam Hasan (a) was riding his horse when a man suddenly blocked his way. This man, who had just come from Damascus, did not like the Prophet's family and began saying cruel things to Imam Hasan (a).

When the man finished saying his hurtful words, Imam Hasan (a) got off his horse and smiled at him. He said, "Salaamun Alaikum, O brother. You seem like you are new in town. If you are hungry, let me feed you; if you need something, let me help you. Please come to my home and be my guest."

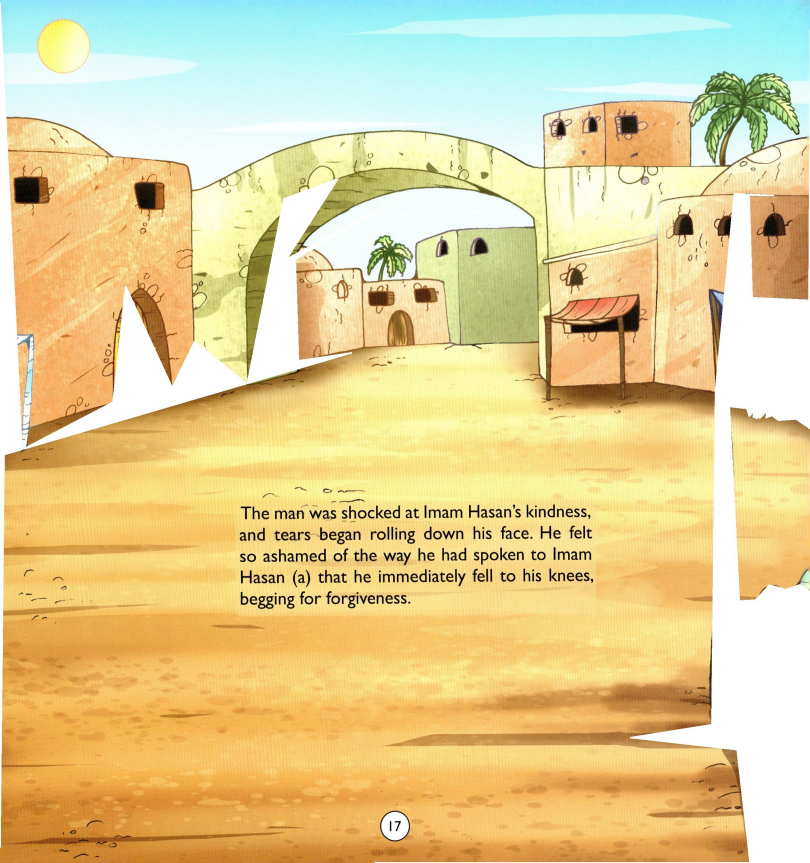

The man was shocked at Imam Hasan's kindness, and tears began rolling down his face. He felt so ashamed of the way he had spoken to Imam Hasan (a) that he immediately fell to his knees, begging for forgiveness.

Imam Hasan's kindness did not stop there. He was even kind to animals! One day, while he was eating, a hungry dog came and sat in front of him. Imam Hasan (a) began to tear pieces off of his bread to share with the dog.

One of his companions was walking by and looked surprised to see the Imam (a) feeding the dog. He asked, "O Imam Hasan (a), is this dog bothering you? Should I take him away so that you can finish eating in peace?"

The Imam (a) replied, "No, please let him be."

His companion looked surprised and asked, "Why, O son of Rasulullah (s)?"

Imam Hasan (a) gently answered, "I would feel ashamed before Allah if I eat from His blessings while a hungry creature is looking at me and I do not share."

It is said that every morning, Imam Hasan (a) would spread out a large carpet in front of his house where he would sit and offer to help all the poor people who were passing by. It would get *so* crowded outside his home that they would have to close down the street!

Others would come just to admire his beautiful face because it would remind them of Rasulullah (s). And as they watched him help the poor so lovingly, they were reminded of the generosity of Rasulullah (s).

May the peace and blessings of Allah be upon Imam Hasan al-Mujtaba (a), who truly lived up to his name: the best of good-doers.

Biḥār ul-Anwār, Vol. 43, P. 238
Biḥār ul-Anwār, Vol. 43, P. 344
Biḥār ul-Anwār, Vol. 43, P. 352